This book was written in honor of my sister Connie
And
Dedicated to my loving children
Chad and Alyssa

Table of Contents

Acknowledgements

This book would not have been possible without the help of so many people throughout my journey. The list of loved ones that prayed for my healing, the many cards and gifts, and the encouragement along the way helped make this happen – helped make me happen. I felt my experience was about a calling that I couldn't foresee, but through divine intervention, it came together with the most infinite of plans. I knew I needed to write a book about my experience but I had no idea where to start.

Thanks to Harshajyoti Das' generosity and guidance, a book was born as the result of his gifted blog site -www.healcancer.org. Additionally, I am thankful for my editors; Ed and Rick for helping me produce a quality product.

I am honored to recognize Sharon and Karen (Sharing and Caring) for their love and support - offering me compassion and strength in my darkest hours and Judy and Linda who demonstrated the epitome of grace and understanding through my many peaks and valleys.

I was blessed to be in the presence of many amazing healers – Dixie Yeterian, John of God, and Sara O'Meara were just a few of my spiritual healers. Medical professionals such as Dr. Bays, F. Mehrabani, and Naturopath, Andrew also contributed greatly towards my healing.

I also want to thank all those who challenged me along the way. I had doctors, friends, family and other loved ones who challenged my beliefs. Had it not been for them, maybe I would not have been so determined to prove them wrong.

Finally, I thank God, my Creator, the One, for the opportunity to continue living in the light of the world so I can continue to share the light with which I have been gifted.

Introduction

If you are reading this book, you have either been diagnosed with cancer or you are close to someone who is. Maybe you just want to learn more. Whatever your reason, you are compelled to learn more about the life-threatening disease that has affected so many lives and most importantly – yours. Something inside you has driven you to this point. That is what has brought you here and just like me, I searched for answers in my journey of self-discovery, self-realization and self-healing through the onset of a diagnosis of cancer.

I was diagnosed with squamous cell carcinoma at the base of my tongue in November of 2012. It was the furthest from my thoughts that I would ever be diagnosed with a life-threatening disease such as cancer, even though my dear sister, Connie, had recently been diagnosed with colon cancer a year prior, almost to the date, in November of 2011.

There are so many aspects to cancer – not just the physical damage that occurs, but also the emotional and spiritual aspects. Cancer causes many of us to look deep inside our authentic selves. It causes us to look at our lives and see what is working and more importantly – what is not.

There are many books on cancer but not many that address how it impacts us emotionally. What does one go through when they are diagnosed with a life-threatening illness? Granted, not everyone senses the same thing, but throughout my experience I realized how important it is to one's healing to know that you are not alone in your experience.

During an intimate conversation with my sister while discussing her experience of feeling alone and misunderstood, she commented, "...but, you wouldn't understand." She then paused briefly, and in a very soft, solemn tone of realization she stated, "...actually, you do." In that moment of grace, we both related to our shared feelings and how cancer had affected us both so deeply. It was a pivotal moment for the bonding of two sisters – to know we were not alone.

Through the content of this book, I would like to do the same. I would like you to know that some of the feelings and emotions you are experiencing are normal and most importantly, can bring you to a deeper understanding of your authentic self and hopefully to a greater point of healing.

Throughout the book I reference God, my Almighty Spirit, the One, Infinite Being, the Creator, Universal Spirit – they are all the same to me. Apply whatever term or understanding best serves you in your journey. The key is to understand your connection in hopes it will bring you closer to your own healing. May you be blessed, as I have been, with an inner 'knowing' through this deeply profound experience of my personal awakening.

All is in Purpose and Divine Order

I believe everything happens for a reason. So when I received my diagnosis, I immediately dug into the depths of my soul and thought – there is a reason for all this and I need to find out what it is. One of the many reasons I have determined, is this book. The greatest reason, however, is the ability to experience the journey and come out a better person than I was before. I am a better person because I am healthier – inside and out. It has given me the ability to see and acknowledge the quality of my being and realize my own true self-worth. I wish the same for you. That is why I am sharing my personal experience with cancer.

There are many books available that can be of service to those who are beginning a relationship with cancer, however, I wanted to approach the message in a way that is easy to read, easy to understand and a means that gets us back to the basics – the basics of our ABCs. I pray, that as you relate to the *ABCs of Cancer*, that you will learn more about yourself and the message that cancer (or any life-threatening disease) can offer to the growth of your soul.

This is the first of a series of books that will help you throughout your healing process. My ultimate goal is to help you heal from the inside out. Although there are many techniques and therapies that can assist in healing, I chose to address the emotional side of healing first. I believe that regardless of what other measures and techniques we apply to our healing journey, we must connect with our emotions and allow them to be beneficial versus detrimental. By sharing my thoughts, feelings and emotions, I hope it brings you an understanding and more clarity in your own experience. I pray that it brings you comfort in knowing that you are not alone.

Our journey in this lifetime is not solely for the good of others (as I once thought), but also for the good of ourselves. As we reconnect to the quality of our Being, our inner light shines brighter. I believe that is the true purpose in living our lives - experiencing the highs and lows, surviving the highs and lows, and learning from the highs and lows that ultimately bring us back to our origins – the ABCs of life.

For some, it takes the pillars to shake, the earth to crack, and a diagnosis of a life-threatening disease to wake up and smell the roses. For me, it took cancer to allow my hardened shell to crack, my walls to come down and to finally open the doors of my authentic self to allow my light to shine through.

What will it take for you to shine your inner light?

"And as we let our own light shine, we unconsciously give other people permission to do the same"
Nelson Mandela

"Let there be light"
Genesis 1:3

AWAKENING

AWAKENING begins with earth shattering news that you have cancer. Your eyes have now been opened to a life that you never knew existed – until now. Whatever you knew before this time has all changed. Your life of normalcy is no longer an option. You now have been awakened to the life of living. Yes. You are now waking up to realize that life is a gift. Life is a very fragile gift and you have been given the magnifying glass to see more clearly what your life is all about and what you would like to do with it now that you have a chance to redefine who you are.

Awakening to your new existence is not easy. We want to tightly grasp onto our rose-colored glasses and look the other way in hopes that fate will bypass us as it searches us out. Alas, fate is just as determined as we are. The saying, "you can run but you cannot hide" is prominent when it comes to dealing with a life-threatening ailment.

Awakening is about looking your fears right in the eye and saying, "I see you and I am prepared to deal with whatever it is that I have ignored or refused to see throughout my life". Whatever your fears are, they usually narrow down to one thing – self-love. Cancer gives you the opportunity to determine who you really are by opening your eyes to your world and finding that what honors you and/or that what holds you back from being your true self. If you have been neglecting things in your life that you know you should change but never have, cancer is your opportunity to make those changes.

Now is the time to reflect on the things or people in your life that have given you pleasure and/or pain. Now is the time to determine what and who should remain in your life. Look for things that touch your inner soul and brings you joy. Look for those who bring out your true Self; those who honor, respect, and accept your unique qualities that make you special. Look inside and see the real you. It's time to awaken.

"There is only one time when it is essential to awaken. That time is now."
Buddha

"Your body holds deep wisdom.
Trust in it. Learn from it.
Nourish it.
Watch your life transform and
be healthy.
Bella Bleue

BELIEFS

BELIEFS are what keep you going each and every day. Your belief system is what defines you. So what are your beliefs about cancer? Do you believe that cancer is a life sentence? Do you believe that cancer can be a gift? Depending on your belief system will determine your outcome. There will be highs and lows, ups and downs, but ultimately, it is your core belief system that propels you into your 'after life' sentence of a cancer diagnosis.

I have always had a deep connection with God, the Source, the One, Universe, or whatever represents the inner knowing of my existence. I've always had a quest to understand this connection. I was the child who would hitch rides with the neighbors so I could attend the Presbyterian Sunday School and Service. I was the 6-year-old who actively participated in the neighbor's Latter Day Saints' summer studies so I could expand my understanding. I was also the one who innately knew there was something more than myself and I wanted to feel the connection. I wanted to know God (or whatever term was used depending on the event), so I participated in as many opportunities as possible to nurture my desire to be closer to The One. In spite of my active participation in this life quest, I believe I have never been as close to God as I am now.

I feel I have a deeper understanding and knowing of how God or Source is represented in my life now. Before cancer, or as I refer to the period as BC, it seemed I communicated with God mainly when I was in dire need of support in my relationships or finances. I felt 'spiritual' and fostered my relationships around the good of God. I did my best to follow the Golden Rule – "Do

Unto Others as They Would Do Unto You." I studied many forms of the representation of God as I was baptized Presbyterian, confirmed Lutheran, attended the Catholic Church in my teens and favored the Unity Church as I progressed through the years. I observed many forms of religion and spiritual practices. Eventually, these experiences led me to follow my heart and the inner spirit of God, without the dogma of structured religion. I find it difficult to accept only one religion or spiritual belief that claims one way is better than another, as I believe that we are all One within God and no one religion or belief is better or worse than another, as long as the belief is focused on love. The key is to accept God (or whatever term resonates best with you) in your heart because once you do that, you will find an inner strength and peace that will help carry you through the difficult times.

You do not have to believe in any certain religion. You only need to believe in yourself, just as God does. My belief is what gave me strength. My belief is what gave me hope. I knew God was preparing me for something bigger than myself. I needed to shed the false bravado of organized religion and just allow God in – completely and wholly. When I did that, I connected with my inner knowing and my healing became real.

It doesn't matter what your belief practices are. What is important is that you truly believe in your wholeness and wellbeing. You must believe that you will be healed – regardless of the healing techniques or modalities. You are responsible for accepting your own healing – no one else can do it for you. Once you acknowledge this reality, your real healing will begin.

"BELIEVE"

Believe in Yourself

7 Basic Principles

I am responsible for creating my own
happiness in life
I know and follow my values and principles
on a daily basis
I'm learning and improving with every new
experience
I am capable of overcoming obstacles in my
life
My attitude can permeate all external
conditions
I am willing to make short-term sacrifices for
long-term gratification
Others respect me, and see me as a source of
insight and motivation
Author - Unknown

"Believe your life is worth living and your
belief will help create the fact."
William James

CANCER

CANCER is the inability of our normal cells to die. Each of our cells performs specific functions in our body so it can operate to its peak ability. They perform their duties and then naturally die off (called apoptosis). This natural cell death allows the body to rebuild itself and occurs continuously throughout the body. We are completely unaware of this function as it is continually reforming, redesigning, and renewing itself. Sometimes, however, our body becomes weakened and negatively impacts the healthy cells, causing them to form abnormally. The abnormal cells then fail to naturally die off and instead, they proliferate and grow. This abnormal growth cycle then forms tumors. Sometimes the tumors are benign – which is simply a compilation of cells that have the inability to invade neighboring tissue. These tumors are non-cancerous and are considered non-harmful. The only danger they could cause is if the growth is in an area that impedes another organ or area in the body to function properly. A malignant tumor however, is the representation of abnormal cells bonding together, fighting for space as they continue to grow and multiply. This growth, or metastasis, continues to invade local tissue, organs and other locations in the body. Ultimately, if one were to die, it would be due to the impediment of the body to perform its basic function, not necessarily from cancer.

So what weakens our body to the point where normal cells turn abnormal?

Compromised immune system

Parasites

Chronic bacteria and fungus

Chronic stress
Emotional distress
Viral infections
Lack of desire to live
Excessive use of antibiotics
Toxins

This list is not fully inclusive of the many factors that impact the onset of cancer. Even genetics can play a role. It is good to understand that any of these can affect how our body functions and if we weaken the system, the body can't fight for survival and the abnormal cells eventually take over.

The importance of this information is to know you can experience not only the physical effects from the process of cancer, but also emotional responses. Coping with cancer is quite a daunting task. I have experienced many highs and lows throughout my healing. Many times, even when I knew what was the right response to a certain situation, I still reacted emotionally, I became a basket case of emotional distraught and even though I knew that is not how I wanted to feel, I had no control over my emotions. We will discuss further emotions such as depression, fear and anxiety later in the book but it is important to know how deeply our coping mechanisms operate.

Additionally, some treatments can cause even heightened effects in dealing with cancer. The key to all of this is that there is no right or wrong way of response to your situation, or to the situation of others. This applies to loved ones who are affected by a loved one's diagnosis. Cancer affects everyone.

Some emotions that you may experience are anger, fear, guilt, shame, hopelessness, resentment, loneliness, regret, numbness, grief and possibly suicidal thoughts. You may cry for no specific reason. This is normal. Feeling joy and happiness may be difficult to feel or even unattainable, which adds more sadness to your state of being. All these emotions are normal. The key is to recognize them, let them run their course, and then look for the silver lining. Look for the things that bring you inner peace and joy. Think positive thoughts versus any negative doom and gloom. Trust me – they will be there (the doom and gloom that is). It is normal because we do not know what our future holds – none of us do, but the diagnosis of a possible death sentence takes us reeling down a dark narrow path. Look for the light. Where there is light, no darkness may enter. Remember to focus on the light when you feel those emotions of sadness, grief, or hopelessness try to take over.

As you deal with the emotional responses of your situation, place yourself in God's grace. Look to the light, feel the light and BE the light. This will bring a state of calmness and acceptance that whatever God has planned for you is for your greatest good. Release your life to God and all will be well. We are all perfect and divine Beings and realizing this is a major part of our healing.

Healing Affirmation

*All of my cells know what to do in order to heal.
Every single one of my cells is filled with wellness,
health, and vitality.
I am the picture of positive energy and
well-being.*

Courage....

I savor each moment,
because I do not know
exactly when a heavy gust
or breeze might blow.
Should it be today,
I'll shed my sorrow in a tear
While my courage battles
the uncertainty I fear.
Dreadful emotions,
for which I can't prepare
will likely taunt me
with sporadic despair,
but I'll be patient amid the highs and lows
for that is the process
by which grieving goes.
I will accept my fate in spite of the stress
and strain,
ignoring should'ves, could'ves, would'ves
to rid my pain;
As will the sun's radiance on my thirsty
skin
restore in due time my contented grin.
Maria C. Dawson

DEPRESSION

DEPRESSION is the silent and invisible illness that society can't see. We can't cast it, nor can we mask it. No one wants to talk about it, yet according to the Centers for Disease Control, over 10% of the United States population has experienced depression in their lifetime. This equates to approximately one in every five Americans has firsthand experience with depression or a mood disorder. In 2013, depression was considered a worldwide epidemic. The causes of depression are many, but the propensity for depression is even higher when diagnosed with a life-threatening disease such as cancer.

In my challenges with cancer, I went into a state of deep depression that ultimately hindered my ability to heal. I knew this, which added to my on-going state of depression. Depression can strike overnight or gradually, which shadows its blatant impact and damage to the personal psyche. When I was in the state of depression, I didn't want to eat, although I knew I needed to. I didn't want to visit with my friends as I felt I had to put on a positive image for them and that felt hypocritical to me. I couldn't enjoy anything. I managed to function, but minimally. I went to counseling but only to put on a façade for the counselor to help me get through the long hour. I had plenty of family and friends that supported me but their love and encouragement seemed to fall on deaf ears while I was suffering from depression.

Depression caused me to go inward but not in a positive way. I entertained the negative thoughts and beliefs and it created an ongoing cycle of shame, guilt, anger, pain, heartache, and lethargy.

I recall sitting in my backyard one day, trying to apply the positive reinforcement I had been given to enjoy nature and all of God's gifts. While I was in the state of depression, I couldn't see through the clouds. My vision was dark and dreary and as this darkness reigned over me, I sunk even deeper because I knew that was not who I was.

If you or someone else is suffering from depression, it is important to address it and get help. It may not necessarily be the exact kind of support you need at the time, but every little bit of support helps. Once we can push beyond the threshold of darkness that quietly looms over us and lift the veil of illusion, we can then regain our appreciation for life and find gratitude in all that is.

What finally brought me out of my depression was my connection to God. I finally accepted His love which in turn allowed me to love myself. I finally found value in my existence. I may have known it all along, but I don't think I believed in my value and worth. (See how important belief is!) Once I began believing in my Self, I began to see the value in all of God's beauty. I could finally enjoy watching the sun rise and the grass grow once again. So often we take things for granted. I didn't think I did until I sunk into a state of depression and then I could not appreciate anything.

Depression is a physiological state that affects our emotions. It is basically a chemical imbalance in our system that affects the neurological transmitters in our brain. When we understand this, we can better understand our emotions that seem completely contradictive of whom we really are. Because it is a chemical imbalance, we can treat it through a number of techniques or therapies. Many physicians may suggest pharmaceutical remedies. I prefer, however, to treat the imbalance with proper diet, supplements, breathing techniques, exercise, energy practice, and meditation whether through prayer or ritual. Physical touch also helps treat a chemical imbalance through the release of much needed endorphins.

Don't forget the loving beings in your lives. Our animals – the ones that love you no matter what. They are there for your comfort, so allow them into your life to help you heal. They will help you heal by remaining by your side throughout the ups and downs, the highs and lows and the tears and the laughter. They will lick your hand when no one else knows your inner pain or sadness. Remember, they are here for you – they are here for all of us.

"Animals are the bridge between us and the beauty of all this is natural. They show us what's missing in our lives, and how to love ourselves more completely and unconditionally. They connect us back to who we are, and to the purpose of why we're here."
- Trisha McCagh

ENERGY

ENERGY healing is very important when healing from a disease or chronic illness. Albert Einstein knew exactly what he was doing when he stated, "Everything is energy and that's all there is. Match the frequency of the reality you want and you cannot help but get that reality. It can be no other way. This is not philosophy. This is physics." He additionally was quoted as saying, "Energy cannot be created or destroyed. It can only be changed from one form to another."

To apply this to cancer, we must understand the frequency cancer represents through our emotions. According to Dr. David R. Hawkins in Power vs. Force, he addresses the variant levels of frequencies that emotions hold in our bodies. If we are feeling despair, regret or blame, our levels are very low (30-75), whereas if we are feeling joy and love, our levels are (500-540). In order to maintain a healing energy system, we need to maintain a frequency of 200+. In addition to our emotional frequencies, we can monitor our physical energy, which in actuality is a result of our emotional frequencies. If I am depressed or sad, I will reflect a low frequency which fosters the environment for cancer. If I am happy and full of joy, it is difficult for a disease to survive. We can't always force ourselves to be happy or in the state of joy, so it is important to understand other healing modalities that can help raise our vibrational levels to higher frequencies.

Meditation can bring our bodies into a heightened state of bliss and naturally raise our frequency. For those of you who find it difficult to meditate, sitting in nature or listening to music that resonates with you and brings you happiness can help raise your frequency. Find what makes you feel good and apply it to your daily routine. This will greatly benefit your healing.

Hands-on healing is also very conducive to the healing process. The use of Reiki, Acupuncture, Crystal Healing, and Quantum Healing are some common forms of energy healing. These forms of healing go deep into the body and into the cells. The effects are not immediate, so it is important to continue a routine of energy healing to get to the core of imbalance in the body. Because everything is energy, our body can feasibly heal itself of any ailment by assisting it in raising the frequency of the impairment.

Studies in Chinese medicine show doctors raising the energy through chanting and you can literally watch them shrink a tumor as shown in the attached You Tube link: https://m.youtube.com/watch?atuoplay=1&v=HecA7XRO7eQ. Energy healing is powerful.

By understanding its power, you must also realize it can go two ways – positive or negative. That is how cancer begins. Through lower energy, it resides in the body. Depending on where it resides may indicate a deeper meaning also. Louise L. Hay wrote a book, *You can Heal Your Life*. She explains that the different parts of the body reflect our inner thoughts, emotions and beliefs. As an example, my cancer was in my throat. This is the location of my fifth chakra, an energy point that represents communication. So when I was diagnosed, I immediately knew I was not fully communicating what I felt inside or who I really am. I found that a bit challenging as I am a fairly open communicator. The key here is that I considered myself 'fairly open'. What inner thoughts am I holding back? Am I in fear of judgement, rejection or ridicule if I speak my truths?

Additionally, there is a saying that the longest, yet most difficult journey we will ever take is the 17 inches between our head and our heart. This resonated deeply with me because I am always thinking. My thoughts are on overload, which hinders my ability to connect to my heart and simply listen to what my heart is saying. I believe the location of my cancer was an opportunity for me to bridge my head and heart and rather than approach everything in a logical manner, it is crucial to my existence to stop and listen to what my heart is saying and simply, follow my heart.

There are a number of other books that help you look into the location of your ailments and see what the body is trying to tell you. Another recommendation to learn about your body and its messages is *When Your Body Says No* by Gabor Mate M.D. The body offers us many signs, many hints to help us get back into balance and achieve homeostasis, which is the body's ability to perform at its best. Listening to our body is one of the greatest gifts we can offer ourselves and our healing.

"Your body holds deep wisdom.
Trust in it.
Learn from it. Nourish it.
Watch your life
transform and be healthy."
Bella Bleue

Perfections

"Listen as your heart and
soul speak.
Squint with your ears.
Smell through the tips of
your fingers.
Taste every tone and
listen for every tingle,
for it is in your senses that
your body talks to you and
reminds you of your
perfections."

LK Rost

FEAR

FEAR is a powerful four letter word that can cut to the core of our Being and halt our ability to heal. Fear is our enemy and once we recognize its power, we can learn from it, turn it into strength and master that which attempted to render us crippled and defenseless. Fear teaches us to dig inside ourselves, turn on the spot light, and examine exactly what is holding us back from our true knowing - our true endeavors - our true, authentic selves.

When diagnosed with a life-threatening illness, it is common to feel all our fears rise from within. What are your fears? Are you afraid of dying? What does that mean to you? Are you worried that if you die, how will your loved ones carry on without you? Are you afraid that you won't be missed or that you failed to leave a mark in the world? Are you afraid that your life was all for nothing? Are you afraid of leaving this world too soon because you never finished what you set out to do? Are you afraid of suffering from the effects of your illness or worse yet, the effects of the treatments? What are your inner most fears?

Fear is a very real emotion and it causes us to rise or fall. If we fall into the arms of fear, we can't move forward. Many times we can be frozen in fear and simply not move and like a pond of water that doesn't move - it becomes stagnant.

We can learn from fear, however, and use its power to our advantage. By reflecting into what we fear most, we can slowly peel back the layers and see what is truly holding us back from our authentic selves. We can then see it for what it is and move forward. We can sever the connection to the heavy anchor that has kept us from sailing. All we have to do is face our fears.

One of my biggest fears in my relationship with cancer wasn't whether I would be healed or not, but more about suffering from the effects of the disease. Because it was located in the throat, it caused a number of issues for me such as limited swallowing, eating, and breathing. What's THAT about? That is about my lack of love for life and I was literally cutting off my ability to feed not just my body, but my soul. I feared that I had not lived my life to the fullest and frankly, that was true. I hadn't fulfilled my life purpose. The universe has a way of guiding us to our greatest good and if we ignore the signs, it can put a number on you. That's when cancer likes to show up.

I recall waking one day and I could barely stand. I was extremely dizzy and I thought, oh no, this is it. It is my time. I fell to my knees and cried. I was so disappointed that I didn't get to finish all the things I had set out to do. I was also very concerned that I had left my kids with the responsibility of going through all my years of clutter. What a project it would be for them! It's funny, the things that we think about when we think it is our time.

Fortunately, it was not my time and it helped me realize that I needed to stick around longer so I could accomplish the many things I am here to accomplish. Or so I thought.

Life isn't about a checklist of the things we are here to accomplish. It is actually enjoying the process as we venture through our lives. If we live in fear, responding only to that which drives us away from pain or suffering, or draws to false impressions of comfort for fear we will be unloved or alone; then we are making choices out of fear. Any decision made out of fear is not the most beneficial for us. What is the opposite of fear? Love. We will have better outcomes if we make our decisions out of love.

Many times we are presented with news that puts us into a huge state of fear. A diagnosis of cancer is one of them. Too often we are driven to make decisions because we are told that if we don't agree to a certain procedure (such as surgery, radiation treatment or chemotherapy), then the cancer will spread and we will die a horrendous death. How does the doctor know how we will die? From my observances, I have seen and personally experienced more suffering from allopathic treatments than worrying about a peaceful transition. By using the fear of death, we make decisions that can cause us more pain and suffering than the actual disease itself.

Not knowing the future is very frightening, but that is when we have to give up our need for control, or the perception of control. Most everything that exists is beyond our control. We need to accept and let go. Let go and let God take charge.

We are given many opportunities to make life-altering decisions. We actually do this every day, but because many of our actions are routine, we don't realize that a left turn can produce a totally different outcome than a right turn. It is that simple, however, many of our decisions are based on logic.

Doctors may give you a prognosis of 6 months to live (as was determined in my case). This is usually based on statistical data from previous cases however, each case is unique. Your length of life is determined on you and you alone. No one can predict the length of your life, but this is a common scare tactic that doctors use to get us to do what they believe is the right thing to do. I received a message stating I had 6 months to live if I didn't proceed with their prescribed treatment plan of radiation and chemotherapy. Solid in my beliefs, I did not succumb to their fear tactics. I proceeded with my own natural protocol and it wasn't until two and a half years later I agreed to a limited amount of radiation (half of what they suggested) to fully shrink the tumors that were growing in my throat. I made the decision not out of fear, but out of knowing what was in my heart. I agreed to the realization that I could allow 'some' radiation to assist in my healing. Although this was against all my core healing beliefs, I listened to my heart and allowed God to divinely guide me. That heartfelt (not head-feared) decision was crucial to my full recovery from cancer.

As you proceed through life and are given opportunities to make life-altering decisions, ask yourself what are you afraid of? What fear is keeping you from your inner truth and achieving your innermost desires? Listen to your heart and you will hear the right answer and whatever that answer is, know that it is the gentle whisper of your inner knowing, your inner guidance, leading you to what is in your best and highest good. Choose love over fear. Through love and knowledge you will always have the greatest results.

"Fear is the path to the dark side.
Fear leads to anger,
Anger leads to hate,
Hate leads to suffering."
Yoda

"The whole secret
of existence
is to have
no fear."
Buddha

"He
Who overcomes
His fears
Will truly
Be
Free."
Aristotle

GRATITUDE

GRATITUDE is God's gift of Grace. It is operating at our highest level of understanding and acceptance. It is about our attitude in accepting everything that comes our way with a deep understanding of the bigger picture. It is the realization that life is a gift and we are fortunate to have the opportunity to serve the greater good – the opportunity to think and act beyond our selves.

When we are in a state of grief, pain, or fear, it is very difficult to find gratitude in our situation. Too often we feel we have been violated by an illness that is taking our gift of life. We assume that we are to live a long life and the onset of a serious illness is stealing this opportunity for longevity. In reality however, we are given a death sentence the day we are born. It is up to us how we wish to experience our lives and possibly because of our choices, we are dealing with a life-threatening diagnosis. This is very possible, but not always the case. Regardless of the reason behind our condition, we must find the silver lining.

When I attended a local cancer support group meeting, I announced my gratitude for my diagnosis. As incongruent as that may sound, it was true. The diagnosis forced me to look at myself in the mirror and admit what is out of balance in my life. Rather than focusing on the woes of my life, it forced me to focus on the light that shines upon me and within me each and every day.

I didn't accomplish this wonderful state of being overnight. I had to peel each layer of protection back and look at it with the intention to truly dissect its value and benefit to my life. If it did not bring me a feeling of peace or comfort, then I had to evaluate its presence and determine if it was helping me or hurting me. This was a very difficult task, as that meant I needed to review my relationships, especially the ones that were the closest to me – my family and former spouse. Once I came into clarity of the value of these relationships, I could then appreciate their presence in my life. For some, it meant limiting the amount of interaction. For others it meant severing the relationship completely. And for some, it meant cultivating an even deeper relationship. I will go into more depth about relationships later in the book, but the clear message is what Wayne Dyer so poignantly expressed, "If you change the way you look at things, the things you look at change."

So what are you grateful for? How can you find a silver lining in a life-threatening diagnosis?

I ask that you take a few minutes each day as you wake and begin listing things for which you are grateful. Then, as you retire in the evening, reflect back on the day and count the many things, people and events that you can feel the blessings for their presence in your day. Then speak your words of gratitude out loud. Speak them into the ethers and your gratitude will be heard and eventually you will begin to 'feel' your gratitude versus just reciting the words. As you change your perspective, the universe will respond and you will begin receiving gratitude from others. It then becomes a reciprocal effect and the energy of grace will continue to spread. Remember, gratitude is an attitude. Think with positive gratefulness for everything – even the most challenging of experiences. As my spiritual mentor, Dixie Yeterian would say, "It is not the events in our lives that are so important, but our response to the events. THAT is the greatest importance."

"When you meet obstacles with gratitude,
your perception starts to shift,
resistance loses its power,
and grace finds a home
within you."

OPRAH

"Gratitude makes sense of our
past
Brings peace for today
And
Creates a vision
For
tomorrow.
Melody Beattie

HOPE

HOPE and faith was my foundation to healing. Without hope, there is nothing to grab onto, nothing to wake to each day. Hope can be difficult to find when you are experiencing the highs and lows of a medical condition. Our emotions become an untethered ship at sea as we move with each ebb and flow of the many pieces of information that flows our way. It is like we are on a rollercoaster. One minute we feel excited and hopeful because we got a good report from the doctor or we felt really good that day. Then, it can all change on a dime as challenges come our way – whether with the illness or various events in our lives. We can be a pin cushion and if we are not on stable ground living through grace and gratitude, we respond emotionally to every wind that passes our way. It is very difficult to remain untethered in a vast ocean and still expect to keep the boat from rocking. This is where we find anchors that represent hope versus hopelessness. It is very important to look for the silver lining in everything. There seems to be a common reference to the silver lining but it is extremely important when it comes to our survival.

What brought me much comfort and hope – via my analytical mind, was the amount of data I found on the internet. When my doctor first informed me of my diagnosis, he told me to make my healing my full time job. I obeyed his 'prescriptive orders' and set out to learn as much about my condition as possible. This was a very crucial decision on my behalf and was instrumental for my survival. Too often I met up against opponents who didn't support my chosen path of healing through integrative and naturopathic medicine. At first it was quite daunting to listen to those whom I loved and respected, telling me my choices were unfounded, yet I stood steadfast in my belief and knowing I was doing what was right for me and my healing. I was set out to get to the source of the cancer so I would not only heal, but never get it back again. That was my mission and that was my new full time job.

As I learned more and more about cancer, I proceeded to take on a team of professionals that help me in my progress. The team included my ENT, an acupuncturist, numerous practitioners skilled in energy healing, a practitioner skilled in herbal healing, a qigong instructor, a surgical dentist, a compound pharmacist, a naturopath doctor, many dear supportive friends, a confidant who listened to my deepest, darkest secrets and reluctantly, my final physician, an oncologist. It was necessary for me to build my team as each one of them brought something to my healing process.

I noticed that just when I was feeling a bit less hopeful, I would either do further research or I would contact one of my team members and inquire about specific support for my needs at the time. It was amazing how each played an important role in my success. I must admit the least amount of hope was during my experience with the oncologist. I reluctantly agreed to radiation treatment because my air passages were becoming more and more limited to the point I was recommended for a tracheotomy.

It seemed I was the least hopeful when I was in pain. Pain put me into the state of depression and it was difficult to find the silver lining. If you are suffering from pain, I suggest contacting someone on your healing team that can bring you some relief. This is very important in the healing process.

I listened to positive comments from my friends and those who were part of my healing team. I read articles and medical publications that described my condition and through research I would gather information to present to my applicable practitioners to help me determine what supplement was best for me at the time. It was quite challenging but I always had hope residing deep inside me.

Numerous times I would reassure my physicians through my insightful, encouraging reply to their not-so-positive outlook, "keep the faith Doc!" I'm not sure who found that more reassuring – me or my doctors. It was crucial that I could find hope each and every day of my healing.

I can't say that my approach can provide you the same amount of comfort that it provided me but find something that can. Listen to what your body tells you. Don't listen to your mind. What gives you that warm, comfort feeling which I call hope? Grasp onto that feeling. Believe in you, as no one can believe in you more than your Self.

"The natural flights of the human mind are not from pleasure to pleasure, but from hope to hope."
Samuel Johnson

"Some days you will be the
light for others,
and some days you will
need some light from them.
As long as there is light,
there is hope, and there is a
way."
Jennifer Gayle

I AM

I AM......How would you complete this sentence? I am happy, sad, depressed, lonely, regretful, supported, insightful, inspired, blessed and healthy. These are just a few options that you could use to complete this sentence. It is very important how you finish the sentence however, because the power of 'I am' is the power of God. 'I am' is the name of God, the Universal Source. It is considered the lost word, but it is not really lost, in fact it is gravely misunderstood. 'I am' is really who you are. It defines the core of your being. Whatever you place after 'I am' is what you truly believe about your Self. These two words carry such great power and unfortunately, it is often overlooked or undervalued. Whatever words you follow with 'I am' carries the energy of the One and thus, will be reinforced through the power of God. Words have meaning much more than we realize. I often find myself correcting those who talk negatively about themselves and others, explaining to them the power of their words.

The old nursery rhyme, "Sticks and stones may break my bones, but words will never hurt me," is quite a misnomer. Words do hurt, regardless of whether they are words that we place upon others or ourselves. Think about it. When you were a child, do you recall chanting the rhyme or hearing others chant it? Were you by chance, a victim of the cruelty of others by calling you something unbecoming of whom you really were? You may have replied in retribution for the verbal abuse, claiming that it did not affect you, but deep inside, there may have been a sadness or hurt feeling that festered. You may not have admitted it to others, or even yourself, but most likely it was there. This is how powerful words are.

By taking this example into consideration, pay attention to your words. Do you ever criticize yourself? Do you downplay your abilities? If you are guilty of this type of behavior, I strongly suggest you rephrase your thoughts and in turn, rephrase your words. Turn your words into positive energy. BE the words you speak. When it comes to your health, be creative in ways that you can describe your healing such as: I am getting stronger every day. I am feeling better and better each minute, hour and day. I am healing more each and every day. Routine admission of your positive beliefs, create a wonderful foundation from which you can heal.

"I am
happy
healthy
wealthy
and wise
for
I am
blessed."
LK Rost

JOY

JOY comes from within and when we are in a state of unrest, discomfort, and pain – both physical and emotional, it is very difficult to express or feel joy. It makes me think of the saying, "you can't get blood out of a turnip". Meaning, if you don't feel joy inside you, how can you express it?

So what brings you joy? What can you do that puts you in a state of joy? What do you feel when you are in joy? We each have our own path to what makes us feel joy inside, but the important thing is not to invest in and rely on others and their actions to bring you joy. This may happen – say a friend brings you flowers or calls to check up on you. This most likely will bring you joy, but it is not something you can depend on. Too often, we invest our feelings and state of happiness and joy in the actions of others. This is simply setting ourselves up for failure because what happens if we don't get the flowers we were hoping for or if no one has time to check up on us when we are having a bad day? When we become reliant upon the actions of others to bring us joy, we are skating down a slippery slope for disappointment and heartache.

So again I ask, what brings you joy – pure joy? When I was in the depths of my healing, it was very difficult for me to feel joy, let alone describe it. I relied on others to produce the euphoria that I defined as joy. This feeling, as I learned later, was a false perception of joy. It wasn't the real deal. Real joy must come from within. When I learned to let things go and chose not to get caught up in other's actions around me, I no longer became dependent on them as the source of my joy. I no longer made expectations. I released my needs and desires to

God, and that is when my heart opened up to my authentic self and I could actually feel what joy really felt like. This was a wonderful revelation for me.

It seems that when we are given a diagnosis or unexpected news, the wind is taken out of our sails. It is up to us, and only us, to create our own reality so we can sail again. Yes, it is all on our own shoulders. We can no longer hold others accountable for our own limitations.

So one more time – what gives you joy? For me, it is sitting in nature on a warm sunny day, listening to the birds sing. I love to swim also. I enjoy classic rock music and watching certain TV programs that either educate me or just take my attention away from my mind chatter. I feel joy when I am learning and teaching. I feel joy when I am writing. I feel joy when I am around people who appreciate me and express it. I feel joy when I am learning more about my health and the health of others. I feel joy when I can feel God in my heart and feel the love that pours through me. I feel joy when I connect with little children and their innocence. I feel joy when I am dancing. I feel joy when I motivate others. I feel joy when I have helped someone through a difficult time. I feel joy when I look at pictures that remind me of fun times. I feel joy when I am riding on the back of a motorcycle on a barren winding road or a road along the ocean. I feel joy when I can smell gardenias in the wind or fragrant lilacs from the shrubs. There is so much joy around us; we just have to stop, look, smell and listen.

Define your joy and go for it, even if it is one little step at a time. Remember the energy of our emotions. Joy logs in at 540, so raise and keep your energy up through your emotions and continue creating a healing atmosphere for your body. This effort is extremely important to your well-being.

*"Find a place inside where there's joy,
and the joy will burn out the pain."*
Joseph Campbell

*"Happiness happens when you fit with your life,
when you fit so harmoniously that whatsoever you are doing is your joy.*
OSHO

KARMA

KARMA is what many believe is why they have cancer. Maybe they did something wrong and now karma is coming back to bite them in the butt. Although I believe in karma - in the respect of doing unto others as you would have them do unto you, however, to get cancer because of something you may have done in the past is not a belief I hold. The reason I don't believe this is because our actions, no matter good or bad, are reflected through others. That is what I believe is karma. Karma is like a mirror to me. If I am 'good' to others by showing them respect, courtesy, and compassion, then in turn, the universe will provide me with similar experiences. On the other hand, if I am rude, disrespectful and display hate, then I expect that to be reflected back to me. This philosophy has played out in my life, time and time again. That is why I don't think we have gotten cancer because we 'deserved' it due to poor actions of our past.

Cancer is simply a means for our body to tell us that we need to change. We need to look at our lives with honesty and humility and connect with our inner being. We need to ask ourselves what is not working in our lives. THAT is what cancer is about. NOT that we have done someone or something wrong.

If you feel that you are being punished for something you have done, I ask that you look inside and ask for forgiveness because only you can forgive yourself for what you believe has been an injustice. Granted, we do things that may not be as healthy or put ourselves in conditions that foster the onset of cancer, but by no means do these actions, completely cause cancer.

A fine example of this is the heavy smoker who never gets lung cancer and yet there is the person who is diagnosed with lung cancer and they have never smoked a day in their life. What is the reasoning behind that? There is none, especially if you are looking at the actions you take and expect punishment for your actions. There are many factors involved but punishment is not one of them – that is unless you are punishing yourself for actions that you felt were not worthy of the character of your being. That thought alone, could have an impact on whether you get cancer or not.

Our thoughts are extremely important. Where attention goes, energy follows. If we feel shame, guilt, or self-imposed disgust in our actions or thoughts, it can easily manifest into cancer. Be aware of this at all times.

"When you truly understand karma, then you realize you are responsible for everything in your life. It is incredibly empowering to know that your future is in your hands."
Keanu Reeves

LOVE

LOVE is patient, love is kind. We often think of our love for others when we apply love to our lives. The greatest recipient of your love should be yourself. Have you been patient with yourself? Have you been kind? To find the true answers, you may need to step in front of the mirror and ask yourself, "Do I really love myself?" Do I do things for myself just as I would for others? Many times, we place others' needs in front of our own needs. This is what can get us into trouble. We must always take care of our own needs first. It's the same as grabbing your own oxygen mask on the airplane before you place one onto your children. You have to be solid in your own being before you can be there for others.

Do you suffer from this action of helping others before or in spite of yourself? If this is the case, this is one action you should change if you wish to heal from cancer. You can't give from an empty cup and when you are dealing with cancer you should be focused on your own healing before you can help others. You can always give from the saucer but only when your cup overflows. This is not selfishness, this is self-love.

When you look into the mirror, ask yourself, what are you doing to be of service to yourself and well-being? Are you eating well and healthy? Are you sleeping well? Are you exercising enough to keep your body and will strong?

While dealing with cancer, you will need every ounce of fuel – whether through diet and/or exercise. You need the physical strength which will in turn support your emotional strength. These two factors go hand in hand. It is difficult to be strong if you are emotionally depressed and in turn, it is difficult to be emotionally strong if you are not respecting your body and its needs. Remember this - not only throughout your healing, but well after you have been given a cancer-free report.

If you learn how to love yourself, you no longer rely on others to determine your value. You will no longer be dependent on other's actions to determine your worth. The ability to love yourself fully frees you from altered emotions based on the actions of others. This is very important to remember while going through your healing experience. Without self-love, it is very difficult to achieve success – in anything.

"This

above all -

to thine own self,

be true...."

William Shakespeare

MARTYRDOM

MARTYRDOM is simply a means to deny what is happening in our lives and blame our injustices on others. At times, it is just easier to blame others for whatever we feel is wrong in our lives, but this is the furthest means of healing ourselves from whatever we may be suffering. Martyrdom can also be a result of depression and it is so much easier to look away from ourselves versus looking directly at ourselves in the mirror and taking responsibility and acknowledgement for our situation. This is extremely difficult but through self-love, you can overcome the effects of martyrdom and self-pity. Living in agony, anguish, and self-persecution is adding to the negative effects of your condition.

The opposite of martyrdom however, is contentment, joy, happiness, comfort and pleasure. Repeating these words instantly bring my energy up. Try it – voice the words; ANGONY – ANGUISH – ANGER. How does that feel in your body? Does it make you feel like the hopeless character in Winnie the Pooh, Eeyore – expressing only negative thoughts of doom and gloom? Take a look at a picture of Eeyore. His body language speaks volumes – he is sad, depressed, pessimistic, and mopes along as he carries his slumped body. That is what martyrdom does to us when we allow the darkness to slip into our soul.

Voice the words: HAPPINESS – JOY – CONTENTMENT How do these words make you feel? Can you feel the difference? Think of the character Tigger in Winnie the Pooh. His exuberant energy is blatantly expressed in his actions as he loves to bounce. His inability to contain his contagious, outgoing optimism for life is boldly expressed and clearly expressed in his body language.

Pay attention to your body language. How does it express your well-being? How does it speak to others? Do you walk with a sureness in your step or do you shuffle your feet, dragging your 'soles' as you attempt each step?

If you notice you are slumping like Eeyore, try jumping like Tigger. Try skipping and thinking a negative thought at the same time. It doesn't work. Try it! You can't be sad with negative thoughts and skip at the same time. The two just don't work together. And if you decide to take my advice and try a little skipping, know that is also a wonderful benefit to your body to get your blood flowing. When you are slumped, your blood is sluggish. When you are happy, your blood is flowing more freely.

Free the dark clouds of sadness, negativity, and doom and gloom and instead, go out into the sunshine and soak in the joys of life. Be thankful for the opportunity to feel and see the light that shines upon you. Step into your well-being with joy and exuberance and be the better YOU – your life depends on it.

"Anger, blame, and martyrdom are thieves. They steal time, relationships and respect. Personal accountability is the life giver, the thing that fills the soul with esteem and repairs it from the inside out."

Amy Larson

"He is a wise man who does not grieve for the things which he has not, but rejoices for those which he has."
Epictetus

NATURE

NATURE is our silent guide, demonstrating the purity and grace that the Universe has given us as a sacred gift. If we follow nature's path, we can hear the voice of our souls, guiding us to what is right and in alignment with our truest self. Just as the trees bend with the wind, we should lean with the challenges that come our way. If we try to defy the effects of nature, the structure of our spirit will snap, just like a broken twig that fails to bend with the force of nature. The broken half can no longer carry its own weight, dangling from the site of weakness and unable to continue its ability to bear fruit. We are no different.

When we allow ourselves to commune with nature; we open our inner core to its original source of existence. The body revels in excitement through the innate connection that is revealed in nature. There is an unspoken 'oneness' that evolves and it is difficult to allow anything but grace to exist in the presence of nature. Not only do the fruits of nature heal our physical body, but the smells, sounds, and touch of nature also cures our inner soul.

If you find yourself in a state of unrest, connect with the Source and release any imbalances to the keeper of your spirit. Release any emotional impurities that do not serve your highest good and allow nature to enter into your soul and heal. Observe the radiant colors it provides for your enjoyment and pleasure. Smell the unique blessings that arrive as a small breeze fills the air. Touch the roughness of the bark of a nearby tree and know the bark is a form of protection that nature has provided to ensure its longevity. Remember the gifts nature provides for your healing and take full advantage of them. They are there for your benefit, free and available at any time. Just for you.

"Nature itself
is the best physician."
Hippocrates

"Let us try to
recognize
The precious nature
Of each day."
Dalai Lama XIV

"No matter how much it gets abused, the body can restore balance. The first rule is to stop interfering with nature."
Deepak Chopra

"There is a wonderful mythical law of nature that the three things we crave most in life - happiness, freedom and peace of mind - are always attained by giving them to someone else.
Peyton Conway March

"The best remedy for those who are afraid, lonely or unhappy is to go outside, somewhere where they can be quiet, alone with the heavens, nature and God. Because only then does one feel that all is as it should be and that God wishes to see people happy, amidst the simple beauty of nature."
Anne Frank

OWNERSHIP

OWNERSHIP means understanding and accepting what is happening with our body as we allow it to transition to a higher state of existence. If we remain in denial, we can't fully heal because we have not fully acknowledged our existence. Taking ownership means taking charge of your situation. By taking charge of your situation, you are taking the bull by the horns and riding it all the way through life. We can empower ourselves by learning more about our condition and situation. There are many resources available that can be of service to our needs. It is very important to understand what your body is doing. Although many may prefer to blindly proceed without fully understanding what is happening in and to their bodies, this is not fully embracing what is happening and throughout the healing process, we will feel powerless and subject to the emotions and actions of a victim. We are not victims unless we wish to travel the path of self-pity, which limits our ability to heal.

Taking ownership is accepting an opportunity to be a full participant in your healing. My doctor told me to make my healing my full time job. I took his prescription to heart and proceeded to learn everything I could about my condition. I reviewed many options for my healing and learned everything I could that would not only help me heal, but do it safely and effectively. There are many options and therapies to assist in your healing, but unless you fully believe in what you have chosen to help you, it will be difficult to fully survive your condition. Once I embraced my condition, and learned enough to trust what my body was telling me, I used every means I could that assisted in my healing. This action resulted in my presence here and now. It wasn't easy. There were highs and lows and it seemed as though there were more lows than highs. The journey took to me to the depths I could never imagine existed within my own being. It may seem daunting at times and you may think you are not qualified but unless you personally take ownership, you will never fully embrace your healing. That is why I believe many people get diagnosed with cancer more than once in their lives. I believe there are a number of factors involved but your belief about your cancer is one of them and a very important factor. If you heal yourself from the inside out, it should not return.

"You must take responsibility for your own choices & actions, for you learn nothing until you take ownership of your life."
Eon Brown

PHASES

PHASES experienced when diagnosed with cancer can be varied and sporadic, inconsistent and yet common, as the healing process unfolds. In my case, my first reaction was numbness. I felt I was in a 2 day conscious comma, watching the many thoughts flow through my head, yet not understanding any of them as they flew by.

I immediately began to research my condition. I needed to know my options for treatment, healing, recovery, and longevity. I remained in the research stage throughout my healing and still do to this day. It is an on-going job. Healing is not something that you can treat and then just walk away.

Upon diagnosis, you now have entered into a phase of constant patrol. You need to be connected with your body. You need to listen to the many signs your body tells you and above all, trust your inner knowing of what is best for you and your healing. Once reality has settled in and for some, that may never occur – reality that is, but if you are one of those who can look in the mirror and say, ok, it's time to face the music – either I grab an instrument and start playing or I put the violin down and walk away. I have found it is best to pick up the instrument and learn to play.

As noted previously, there is no set pattern of your emotional phases. You establish your own norm. You could remain somber for weeks or appear to be joyful in your situation. I must admit, my joyful moments were far and few and for the most part, I remained separated from the outside world because I didn't want to pretend I was ok, because in reality, I wasn't. I didn't physically feel well and emotionally, I was distraught over my condition. Throughout the healing process, however, I became empowered through knowledge. It seemed just as I felt like giving up, a new piece of information would come my way, and add more options for healing. This gave me hope. Hope is what kept me going.

There were many phases that included sadness, anger at others, blame, remorse for my thoughts and actions, grief, depression, and towards the final point of my recovery, I even got physically aggressive. That seemed to be a turning point for me to finally 'give in' to my reality. I had periodic stints of joy and happiness, but they seemed superficial because I wasn't fully connected to what I would define as my true inner-being. I wasn't in alignment with myself. I was feeling victimized – not necessarily by my diagnosis, rather, by the actions of others. I couldn't understand their lack of compassion for my situation. Eventually I realized that everyone experiences cancer in their own way – whether they are diagnosed or someone close to them is diagnosed. They also experience emotional phases of their own. After months of focusing only on myself, I finally woke up and realized I was not the only one going through the effects of cancer. The sooner you can realize this - that everyone experiences cancer in their own way, the sooner you can get a stronger foothold toward your recovery.

Many times people choose to go the quick route toward healing – surgery, radiation or chemotherapy. This was not my choice. I can honestly say I suffer from the need for immediate gratification, however in this case, I knew it was not my best approach. I wanted to get to the source of my cancer and completely clear it from my system, once and for all, so I didn't have to deal with it and all the intense emotions. It took me three years and in hindsight, 'it was the best of times and it was the worst of times'.

I finally entered into the gratitude phase, which is a wonderful indication of inner healing. As I mentioned previously, you may enter into many different stages – sporadically and inconsistently. If you can enter into the gratitude phase and remain there as much as possible, you can then acknowledge your inner healing. Maybe that is what cancer was about for me – to fully achieve inner grace and gratitude for the gift of life.

"Today, as with every day,
is a new day.
Be sure to remind yourself that it is okay
to be different from yesterday
or not quite ready for tomorrow.
Sometimes we take a step back, regress,
and other times we grow more in one day
than we have in an entire year.
And that is exactly what life is about -
balance and change.
For even the moon has its phases, so why
shouldn't we?"
Becca Lee

QUESTIONS

QUESTIONS bring answers, yet many of us fail to ask the right questions when it comes to dealing with our health. There's the old saying, "You don't know what you don't know," but that is exactly why it is important to gain empowerment through learning about your condition. As a trained interrogator, our questioning techniques were the key to our success. We were taught the basic interrogatives – who, what, where, when, why and how. I suggest applying these basic interrogatives to assist you in your healing journey.

When initially diagnosed with cancer, one of the first questions that came to me was - will this kill me or how long do I have to live? Ironically, no one can really answer that question. The answer is based on a number of factors – the type of cancer, the location of your cancer, the stage of your cancer, etc. The answer is based on statistics but every person is unique and every situation is dependent upon many factors. What I suggest for questions is the following:

What type of cancer do I have?
What are the survival rates according to recent statistics?
What options for treatment are available to me?
What are the effects of the treatments?
How will the treatment affect me and for how long?
What services are available to me throughout this process? (Counseling, dietary, on-call, palliative care, research materials and pamphlets, etc.)
Who represents my care team and what are their job skills?
Whom can I call in an emergency?

Who can I call if I have any questions about my condition as a result of my treatment?

What can I expect to feel from this condition and also the effects of the treatment?

Where can I go for credible information about my condition?

Are there support groups for my condition and if so, when and where do they meet?

What is the best thing I can do for myself to help me in my healing journey?

What will be the impacts on my family to include 2nd and 3rd order effects?

These are just a few questions that I recommend asking. Have them prepared ahead of time so you don't forget to ask them. You may not like the answers you get, like, "you will have lifelong residual effects from your treatment," but being prepared in your journey is not only smart, but empowering.

One question that will probably never be answered is how you got your cancer. Traditional medicine rarely addresses this question simply because they don't know, and often times, they don't care to know. In conventional medicine, the goal is to eradicate the signs of cancer in your body. The allopathic doctors are not concerned about the source or root cause of the cancer. If you go to a Naturopathic or Homeopathic Doctor, they will attempt to get to the source of the cancer to fully clear it from your body; healing you from the inside out versus the outside in.

It is important to understand where you are in your healing process because that is what will empower you toward to a healthy state of being. Obviously, there are no guarantees in your eventual outcome, but if you remain abreast of your condition, you are better prepared to accept what comes your way. When you have options, and are informed of these options, you have more freedom of choice. It is always better to make choices based on facts and information versus no information at all. By empowering yourself through knowledge (knowledge is power), then you know you are actively involved in your healing. I feel that by leaving your fate solely to your doctor, you are not taking responsibility for your outcome. This could be an action of avoidance, which is not conducive to your healing. Be empowered. Ask the right questions. Take charge of your healing. You know your body best. Listen for the subtle signs and your body will guide you in the right direction that is best for you and your healing.

"A good decision
is based on
knowledge,
not numbers."
Plato

RELATIONSHIPS

RELATIONSHIPS, risks, rewards and repercussions all go hand in hand. We don't often think of them as one, yet every relationship we choose has its risks and rewards and at times – repercussions. When it comes to surviving a life-threatening disease, a review of our relationships is crucial. The quality of our relationships plays a huge role in either our success or sadly, our defeat. Many times we do not realize the depth of impact our relationships have on our lives. Think about your first love and how wonderful it felt – that euphoric feeling. Now think about a relationship that didn't work out and how deeply it may have hurt you. Two distinct feelings - both are very powerful. Of course we all prefer the euphoric feeling and energetically, that makes complete sense. Your body is in a heightened state which is conducive to healing. When you are sad or hurt by a breakup, your body is unable to efficiently heal itself. This is just one example of how our relationships affect us, but I would like to take it a step further. What about your family relationships? Did you have a wonderful childhood, feeling loved and admired by your parents and siblings, or did you feel ignored, unnoticed, or disrespected? Whatever you felt, whether it was true or not, as a result of your personal perspective, it all is extremely important and affects your health dramatically. Dr. Ryke Geerd Hamer, German Oncologist, discovered what he termed "The German New Medicine" proving the scientific connection between the psyche, brain, and organs. He determined there is a biological conflict through shock or trauma that results in disease such as cancer. He also found the site for which the illness derives is connected to the nature of the

---

conflict. Louise L. Hay follows this theory of a connection between our thoughts and beliefs and how they impact our health, in her book, *You Can Heal Your Life*. As mentioned previously, Dr. Gabor Mate' explores the connection between stress and disease in his book, *When the Body Says No*. Each of these authors can attest to the impact our relationships have on our psyche and our health. Through realization of this, it is important to review the quality of your relationships including your family, partners (past and present), and even your Self. Your relationship with yourself may be the most important one as it impacts the quality of the relationships throughout your life. If you are unhappy with your choices or where you are in life, you may be expressing this imbalance through your relationships. If you do not honor the quality of your being by accepting situations or relationships that do not honor you, what is that saying to the universe and the universal law of attraction? You are basically confirming your belief in the lack of your self-worth and value.

You express your beliefs in every aspect of your life. Look around you. How is your self-worth represented in your environment? How is your self-worth represented in your relationships? Just because we have family doesn't mean that we have to accept inappropriate or less than quality behavior. If a sibling or relative doesn't recognize and respect the quality of your being, then evaluate your relationship with that sibling or parent. What are the positive qualities? What are the negative qualities? Frankly, this should be done with all your relationships. We think because we are family we have to accept less-than-quality behavior. This is the furthest from the truth. What is important is that you determine what standards you are willing to create in your relationships that will honor you and your values. It is up to you to set boundaries of what you are willing to accept and what you are not. Ultimately, your life depends on your decision to determine your own self-worth and then enforce acceptable behaviors that are in alignment with your personal level of love. It is tough love when you sever a relationship with someone who is not valuing you and your worth. It is divine love, however, when you recognize this because you are demonstrating to the universe your values and confirmation of worthiness. Because of your actions, you will in turn begin fostering nurturing, caring, kind, loving relationships into your life. You will also enhance your health in doing so.

Think of a vibrant flourishing plant that is moved to an area that receives no sunlight and is rarely watered. The plant dwindles and eventually dies. Our bodies are no different. Think of our relationships as our source to sunlight and water. It makes sense to ensure you are self-nurturing and requiring others to do the same. In doing so, you will be rewarded with loving, caring relationships and ultimately, a healthy life.

"The purpose of a relationship is not to have another complete you, but to have another with whom you might share your completeness."
Neale Donald Walsch

SUPPORT

SUPPORT comes in many ways. It often comes in ways that we don't expect and at times, fails to arrive in ways we should expect. When we are ill, we think that our loved ones will be there for us when we need them. Through personal experience, I have learned this is not always true. What we need most during a time of illness, is the compassion and understanding of the situation that we are in and yet, no one can really understand our emotions or our needs unless they are experiencing the same thing. Even then, we all have our individual needs and desires that bring us our greatest comfort. How can someone fully know our needs? It is extremely important to understand that you must rely on your own internal love first and foremost. When we are vulnerable, we can become raw, weak, and critical of both ourselves and of others. This can cause a misunderstanding and become a deterrent to the supporting love that we need to heal.

Years ago, my Pastor once told me, "Do not make expectations, as that leads to failure and disappointment." It took me a while to understand what he meant but through years of personal application, I completely understand. It is difficult not to make expectations of those closest to us. It seems as if it is an unwritten understanding that those closest to us will be able and willing to support us, however, as my Pastor stated, it leads to failure and disappointment.

There are many resources for support beyond us, our family and our friends. It is important to be part of a support group, whether with a formal group that meets routinely or an informal group that shares similar concerns and issues. There is palliative care that should be provided from the onset of your diagnosis. If you have not been introduced to palliative care, ask for it. It represents a team of professionals that help you throughout your healing process. There are workshops and seminars that can be both informative and supportive. There are web sites and blog sites similar to mine – www.healcancer.org that can help provide an insight to others' experiences and possibly your own. All of these resources provide an additional access for healing support. Do not solely rely on your family members to provide what you think you need. They may not be emotionally equipped, as they too, are experiencing the effects of cancer in their own way.

Cancer affects everyone in your life. Remember this throughout your healing journey. Each person reacts differently and to make expectations of them to understand and show the compassion you may need, is not realistic. When you understand this, you can move forward in your healing. Prior to my understanding and application of this awareness, I found it convenient for my need to blame others' actions for hindering my healing. When their actions didn't appear to be supportive or compassionate of my needs and health, I could then blame my condition on those closest to me. Yes, I played the blame game and it wasn't pleasant. It was my coping techniques of trying to deal with a condition in which I had no control. Since I couldn't control my condition, maybe I could find solace in controlling those around me. This approach didn't work and in fact, backfired on me to the point I lost a major amount of support from those who I felt could have provided me the most.

It's easy to find blame, but it isn't conducive to your healing. It doesn't matter if you try to blame others or if you try to blame yourself. Blame is not part of the healing process. If you recognize any behavior on your part that is indicative of the blame game, try to look within and find a place in your heart for acceptance of that which people can offer.

Go to those who provide you the most support and receive it openly and willingly. It may be where you least expect it, but if there is someone who is giving you their sincere supportive effort through phone calls, cards, gifts, emails, or simply a shoulder to cry on, they are the ones you want to lean in to. They are the pillars that will help guide you through your trials and they will be the ones who will carry you to the finish line.

12 Steps for Self-Care

If it feels wrong, don't do it.
Say "exactly" what you mean.
Don't be a people pleaser.
Trust your instincts.
Never speak bad about yourself.
Never give up on your dreams.
Don't be afraid to say "No".
Don't be afraid to say "Yes".
Be KIND to yourself.
Let go of what you can't control.
Stay away from drama & negativity.
LOVE

Author Unknown

TRUTH

TRUTH and trust establishes a foundation for your healing. What is the truth when you are diagnosed with cancer or a life threatening disease? Can you fully trust everything you are being told regarding your condition and treatment options?

Although I am a very trusting individual, I still felt it was important that I apply due diligence to my healthy recovery and healing. I actually received a devastating message on my phone recorder from one of my doctors in the oncology department. I had seen him previously and I was fully briefed on the recommended treatment (chemotherapy and radiation) and the residual effects that could occur from the treatment procedures. It was over a half page long, type written, explaining all the things that could happen to me as a result of the treatments (this was just the radiation list). Of course I was devastated so I elected to wait, do my research and informed him that I would get back with him regarding my decision. Prior to my ability to respond back, however, he contacted me and left a message stating the following, "Ms. Rost, if you do not proceed with our recommended treatment, you will not be alive in six months." When I heard the message, I thought, "Hmmm, is this the new scare tactic they use these days?" How does he know I will die in six months? How can anyone leave a message like that on a phone machine?

Fortunately, I was solid in my ability to discern information that was provided to me and I basically shrugged off the recording. I did save it however. Maybe I'll slip it into my audio book…..That was over three years ago and I did succumb to partial radiation based on what I felt was the right amount to help shrink my tumors and yet do the least amount of damage. I was fortunate as the tumors shrunk completely and I can now swallow comfortably, my hearing is still intact, my salivary glands are functioning, and I can once again, enjoy the taste of food. This may all seem petty, but when those gifts are taken away from you, you realize how important they are to the quality of your life. Many physicians are focused on extending your life rather than ensuring a quality of life. I chose quality over quantity. I chose to trust my instincts over institution and as a result, I have both quantity and quality of life.

Think about the billions of dollars that are spent on research in cancer treatment yet, there is still no 'official' cure? We can send a man to the moon, we can create duplicate species, yet we can't cure a blood disease?

Bottom line - only you know what is best for you. Listen to all your options and then do your research. Ask questions, ask more questions, and then ask more until you feel fully comfortable in your decision in what is best for you and your healing protocol. Trust yourself. Through this internal trust, you will be in a better place for healing. If you leave all the decisions up to your doctor, it may be you paying the price, not him/her. Each person is unique. Each cancer is unique. Bearing this in mind, each treatment plan should be unique and structured for you and your individual case.

"Trust yourself,
you know more
than you think you do."
Benjamin Spock

UNDERSTANDING

UNDERSTANDING your life and your purpose in life is crucial to your survival. When we are diagnosed with a serious or life-threatening illness, it can propel us into a bewilderment of the unimaginable or it may offer us an opportunity to dig deeper into our souls and determine if we are on track with our life purpose or did we take a detour? You may ask why it is so important to know our life purpose and do all we can to fulfill it. The reason your understanding of your life purpose is so important is that it aligns you with your calling. Your body, mind, spirit and soul are in alignment. When you are in alignment, you are in balance and when it comes to your health, you must strive for homeostasis; the physical state in which our biological system functions in a state of equilibrium - balance that results in a heightened state of well-being. When we are ill, our body is simply out of balance.

If we understand that when our body hurts, bleeds, inflames, or produces tumors or excess growth, it is attempting to get our attention so we can find the source and bring our body back into balance. In future volumes in the ABCs of Cancer, this will be discussed in more detail, providing suggestions of complementary alternative medical (CAM) methods, supplements, dietary recommendations and energy work that can be beneficial for your healthy recovery, however, this volume focuses on our emotional balance.

Because our emotions have such a large impact on our well-being, I felt it was important to offer suggestions to assist a cancer patient in their acceptance and understanding of their situation. Without it, there will be continued turmoil and unrest within the body and the body will have difficulty in achieving homeostasis.

I believe all our experiences guide us toward our life purpose. When we are in alignment with our purpose, the rest of the universe follows suit and we feel complete – physically, emotionally and spiritually. When we are out of alignment – just like a car, it is difficult to keep our vehicle on the straight and narrow path. So how do you feel in your body? Does it feel out of alignment? What about your thoughts and emotions? I can almost guarantee they feel out of alignment if you haven't found balance in your understanding of your condition. Then your body creates a domino effect and you begin playing ping pong attempting to adjust as you go, yet you over compensate for one factor, requiring you to readjust your attention to another factor and before long, it gets out of control and very possibly, depression sets in.

If this sounds like you, I suggest you review the section on depression. By applying the recommendations, you can help yourself get on top of the game.

So what is your life purpose? If a thought popped out – without any forethought, this may very likely be your answer. Too much thinking about it clutters the mind and alters the real answer. If you are having difficulty in determining what your life purpose is, then ask yourself, "What do I really enjoy doing? What am I good at? What things that I do make me feel good?" These questions will guide you in the right direction. If you are focused on your true purpose in life, I believe the universe or God will assist you on your path and slowly you will see things beginning to line up for you. It's like the parting of the Red Sea. It could be a universal 'Ah Ha' moment for you. When this occurs, your emotional energy will merge into alignment with your body and your health will begin to improve. Look within for your answers and ask yourself the big question, "what is the next step or action I must take that is in my best and highest good?" Listen and you will hear the answer. Once you hear the answer, let it resonate and then take action. You are the master of your life. Love it and Live it.

"You are the architect of your own destiny;
you are the master of your own fate;
you are behind the steering wheel of your life.
There are no limitations to what you can do, have, or be –
except the limitations you place on yourself by your own thinking."
Brian Tracy

VULNERABILITY

VULNERABILITY is the birthplace of creativity, innovation, and change according to Dr. Brene' Brown. It is essential that we strip away our protective shields and allow the humanness of life to embrace us completely. You can't appreciate the taste of a juicy orange until you peel its outer layer.

When you are in an altered physical state with a disease such as cancer, you become very vulnerable. You are unsure of many things and you can easily go spiraling out of control with nothing to grasp onto. Through understanding and acceptance of the unknown, you eventually become comfortable with and in your vulnerable state. It's the old saying, 'If you can't beat 'em, join 'em." That is the case with your state of vulnerability. As you get more comfortable with it, you begin to go with the flow versus trying to swim upstream. You get creative with your approach to living. You see things differently and you learn to appreciate every little thing life has to offer. You may even become innovative in your methods of coping and understanding. I have witnessed some amazing survivors who chose to take charge of their life versus letting their condition take charge of them. It forced them to be vulnerable however, and eventually comfortable in their new layer of skin. They became empowered through change and you can too. If you embrace each day with a vulnerable, yet empowered approach by creating ways in which you can find grace and gratitude for every moment, your life with change in ways you could never imagine. Be fearless in your quest for life and find ways in which you can enjoy it to the fullest. We are here to enjoy all that is. Carpe Diem!

"Vulnerability is the
birthplace of
creativity, innovation, and
change. It's also the
birthplace of joy, faith and
connection.
To create
is to make something that
has never existed before.
There's nothing more
vulnerable than that."

Dr. Brene' Brown

WORTHINESS

WORTHINESS may be the source of all that is. Knowing we are here for a reason and every moment we spent depleting our true value is a moment wasted in time – a moment we will never be able to get back. So what determines your worthiness? Who determines your worthiness? Only you can answer these questions and only you can look in the mirror and profess your value.

Often times we grow up learning poor habits and beliefs. The smallest of gestures misinterpreted can plant a seed of unworthiness which impacts our whole existence. We may boast that we are worthy, yet if we review our life experience and look around our homes and relationships, there may be an indication of something different.

Too often we place the value of our worthiness in the response of those in our lives. If we are disrespected, we think we are not worthy of respect. If we don't feel loved, we are projecting an energy displaying a lack of worthiness of love. It is the universal law of attraction. We get what we put out.

We can get caught up in our health situation and think we are not worthy of living. Depression can cause you to feel this way but there is nothing further from the truth. We are all worthy of a wonderful life filled with all that we desire. We are all worthy of this, no matter what mistakes we have made in the past or what things people have told us. We are absolutely worthy of all that this world has to offer, we just need to open our hands and hearts and tell the world, "I am ready to receive my gifts because I am worthy." You are worthy of a healthy living. You are worthy of wonderful relationships. You are worthy of a day filled with joy, peace and love. If at any time, you or someone in your life challenges you at this reality, then exchange any negative thoughts with joyful, happy, 'I am worthy' thoughts. Fill your mind and heart with light and love and accept nothing less, as this is the truth that must resonate within you. YOU are worthy. You ARE Worthy. You are WORTHY. Know it and believe it in every cell of your body. You will know when you have truly trusted and believed this statement as your body will respond with wholeness and healing.

"Don't wait for the end of the day.
Love yourself now.
With some love and respect, the time it takes to prepare healthy food, connect with a friend, meditate, go for a walk, do the things you enjoy, is all time well spent. You need and deserve a lot of loving care. Just as small gradual steps can lead you to health.
Be good to yourself."
InspirationalQuotes.Club

"I believe that owning our worthiness is the act of acknowledging that
We are sacred.
Perhaps embracing vulnerability and overcoming numbing is ultimately about the care and feeding of our spirits.
Brene' Brown

X-RAY

X-RAYS, MRIs, CT scans, PET scans, and Ultrasound tests are medical measures used to determine if cancer is still in the body. These tests can be a source of hope or a source of sorrow. We become dependent on these reports to determine our progress or the lack of progress and we become reliant upon the outcome. From my experience and the observation of many others, the tests can be misinterpreted, erroneous or simply false indications of signs of cancer in the body. It seems archaic to me but these are the basic means for which the system relies upon to determine your state of health. Because of the importance they are given, we consider the results as gospel and if the results are less than positive, it can affect our psyche and spirit dramatically. Because of this, I suggest a mental preparation prior to any exam: picture nothing but positive results, see your Self healed and see your Self smiling. Go into the emotions you feel when you receive positive news. Resonate with those feelings. Think nothing but positive thoughts and regardless of the results of your reports, you with find more hope, faith and peace in your well-being.

If we realized all this is an illusion – we wouldn't get so emotionally distraught over what the doctors are telling us about our bodies. When I went in for a routine appointment, my ENT doctor performed his routine scope of my throat cavity where the original tumor resided. When he scoped my throat and found nothing, he was in amazement because just 30 days prior he was scheduling me for a tentative tracheotomy appointment. When he viewed my throat and found no evidence of any cancer tumor, without forethought, he exclaimed, "It's as if there was never anything there!" I smiled as I listened to his innocent observation. I thought to myself. You are right doc. It is as if there was never anything there and maybe we all created this drama so I could examine my life and get back on track with my life's purpose. It made me think of the classic Christmas movie, *It's a Wonderful Life*. It IS a wonderful life and it took a diagnosis of cancer for me to wake up and remember this simple realization.

"*Reality is merely an illusion, albeit a very persistent one.*"
Einstein

YESTERDAY

YESTERDAY has come and gone, never to return again. Today is here. Therefore, it is important to understand that what we do today can impact what happens tomorrow. Live in the moment, but prepare for tomorrow. Release the yesterdays, for they will never come again. Relish in the thought of knowing you have a chance to recreate a new day – each and every day. The choice is yours to determine if the day will be a wonderful, productive positive day or something less. Make the most of your life – regardless of how long you think it should be. We should live each day as if it was our last and the diagnosis of cancer helps put this into perspective. The moment we are born, we begin our dying process.

So what is the purpose of your life? To play it out as long as you possibly can? What is more important to you – the quantity of your life or the quality of your life? My doctors were perplexed when I challenged them with the choice of a quality of life. If I only had one day to live, I prefer living it in a state of happiness and joy versus living longer under a state of misery, pain and grief. This is my personal perspective and I am sure it is also many others. What is your choice? If you can live with the understanding that we begin dying the day we are born, then each day is extra credit. We are given another day to offer the best of who we are. Are you offering the best of who you are? You may reflect on this thought and think, "Maybe I could offer more and give more of my time. Maybe I could volunteer and offer to those less fortunate". If you are so inclined, take the initiative to serve at your local Salvation Army Center.

Volunteer to serve meals to those in need. You will be humbled. Maybe you could even offer more attention to those closest to you such as a family member or a neighbor. Ultimately, that which you offer comes back tenfold.

Finally, you may realize the most important person in your life is your Self. Realizing this, you should first and foremost, offer your greatest love to your Self. You should offer truth and honesty through self-reflection and then determine how you can improve the quality of your BEing and reflect your light to others. If each of us did this, not only would the world be a better place to live in, but we would truly enjoy our lives and each other. So live for today as if it were your last and express it as if it were your first – because it is.

"Yesterday,
Everything seems so far away..."
Beetles

"Yesterday's
the past,
tomorrow's
the future,
but today
is a gift.
That is why it's called
the
present."

Bil Keane

ZEAL

ZEAL is what is required to overcome the obstacles that come your way as you journey through your healing process with cancer. A simple four letter word, yet it is extremely challenging to express and experience if you are not in the right frame of mind and spirit. It is defined in the dictionary as "a great energy or enthusiasm in pursuit of a cause or an objective." When we focus on the prize, we can approach our healing with zeal rather than responding to every valley that detours us from our deepest intentions. This is the state you should be in to fully heal from cancer or any other life-threatening disease. It is necessary to take the bull by the horns and approach life with zeal, showing desire to live by doing everything possible to improve your quality of life. This means making room for positive situations and people in your life and removing the negative factors that limit you and keep you down.

In the Army, we have a saying, "Stay Alert, Stay Alive." Never did I think I would apply it to a diagnosis of cancer, but having gone through my healing experience, I believe it was my awareness - my attention to the details of my thoughts and the subtle physical warning signs that gave me the clues to what my body needed to stay alive and thrive. You too can rise to the occasion. This is your grand illusion and you are the creator. As we say in the Army, "Be All You Can Be".

"Live life with zeal -
this will help you heal"
LK Rost

CLOSING

I close with the addition of one last story about a motto with which I consistently haunted my doctor during my many appointments. I continued to offer him hope in my healing process by expressing what I knew deep within my soul and that was a complete healing from the inside out. My words once again rang true as I joyfully departed my final doctor's visit. The pristine clinical hallways resonated with my prophetic words while I declared for the last time, "Keep the faith Doc!"

I say the same to you as you journey through your experience. Know that all is in purpose and all is in divine order. Don't let a diagnosis of cancer stop you from living.

This is not the end, rather just the beginning.

*"Keep looking up....
That's the
secret of life..."*
Snoopy

ABOUT THE AUTHOR

Lucinda (Cindy) Rost has a diverse background and a quest to share the light with as many individuals as possible. She retired from the Army and served 22 years as an Interrogator and Educator. While this may seem incongruent with her spiritual gifts, it gave her the opportunity to learn about people from many walks of life - but most importantly, the opportunity to learn more about herself and her inner strengths.

Her extensive background includes numerous degrees including an AAS in Intelligence Operations, BS in Liberal Arts and Metaphysical Science, and completing her MLS with a focus in Integrative Oncology. She is a certified Master Fitness Trainer, Integrative Nutrition Health Coach, and Natural Health Consultant. Her metaphysical studies include Energy Clearing & Healing, Tongue & Fingernail Analysis, Aura Visualization, Regression Skills, Universal Symbology, and Soul Evolvement.

Her future goals are to continue helping others through her writing and to serve as a Naturopathic Physician.

Made in the USA
San Bernardino, CA
13 June 2016